THE STORY OF WORCESTER CATHEDRAL AND ITS PEOPLE

Cathedral Guides

Cathedral Guide

and its artefacts through the lives of the people who have lived and worshipped on this holy site for thirteen centuries. It is the story of kings and princes – of King John, represented as medieval tradition required in the prime of his life by the effigy in the Quire of the Cathedral, and of Prince Arthur, whose chantry chapel heard the prayers of many for one who died at the young age of sixteen. It is the story of rich and poor, of wealthy Worcester men and women of the past, like Mr and Mrs Wylde, and common country folk, depicted in their common activities on the underside of misericords. It is the story of saints, such as Oswald and Wulfstan, of scholars and illuminated manuscripts, of a past Benedictine monastic community, of soldiers and their chaplain, Woodbine Willie. Just as importantly, it is the story of a present community, their worship and service of their neighbours rooted in the past, expressed anew in the present and, through God's love, hopeful for the future. These are several stories and yet they are one, all finding their beginning and their end in the one God, Father, Son and Holy Spirit.

Left: The Nave, looking west from the centre of the Cathedral. The length and width of the Nave have not changed since the 12th century. The ceiling was vaulted in c.1377.

Above: Looking east through the Quire. The brass lectern is shaped like an eagle, the symbol of St John. It stands on an orb, and carries a Bible on its wings.

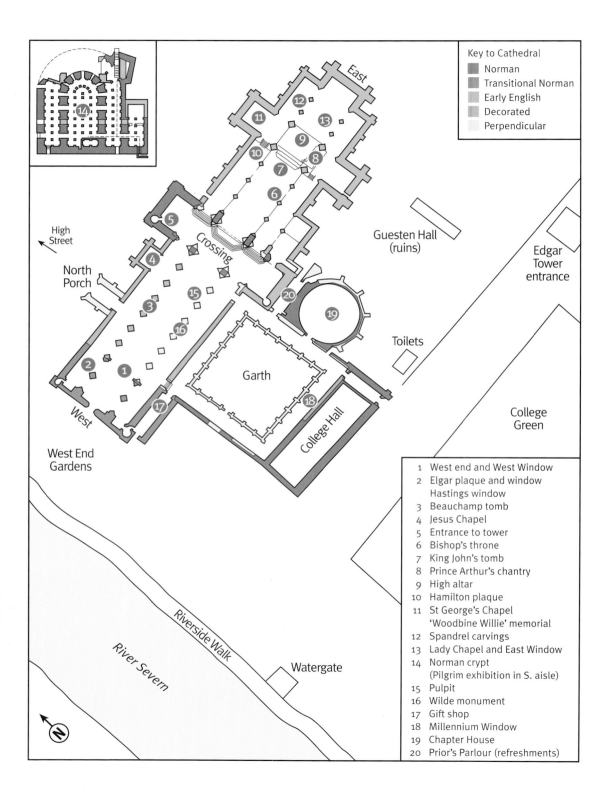

Key to Cathedral
- Norman
- Transitional Norman
- Early English
- Decorated
- Perpendicular

High Street

North Porch

Crossing

East

Guesten Hall (ruins)

Edgar Tower entrance

Toilets

Garth

College Hall

College Green

West

West End Gardens

Riverside Walk

River Severn

Watergate

N

1 West end and West Window
2 Elgar plaque and window
   Hastings window
3 Beauchamp tomb
4 Jesus Chapel
5 Entrance to tower
6 Bishop's throne
7 King John's tomb
8 Prince Arthur's chantry
9 High altar
10 Hamilton plaque
11 St George's Chapel
   'Woodbine Willie' memorial
12 Spandrel carvings
13 Lady Chapel and East Window
14 Norman crypt
   (Pilgrim exhibition in S. aisle)
15 Pulpit
16 Wilde monument
17 Gift shop
18 Millennium Window
19 Chapter House
20 Prior's Parlour (refreshments)

Right: Aerial view of
Worcester Cathedral and city
in 1927, from the southwest.
The layout of the monastic
buildings to the south and
west of the Cathedral is
clearly visible.

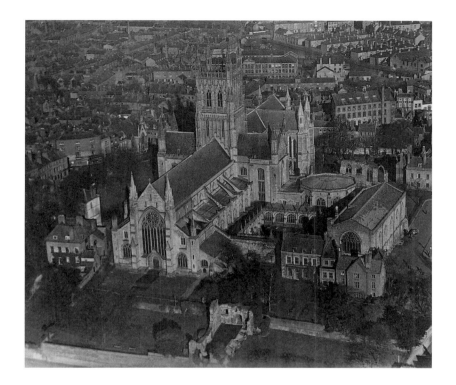

Below: Cross-section of the
Cathedral in 1823, from the north.

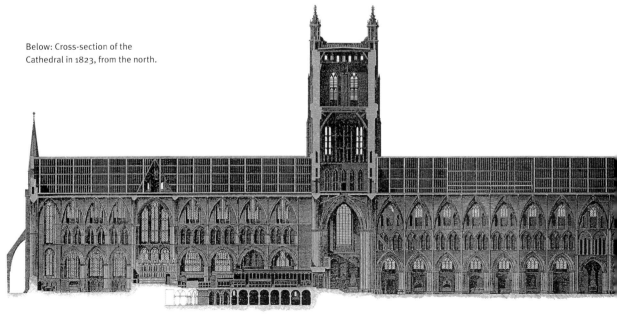

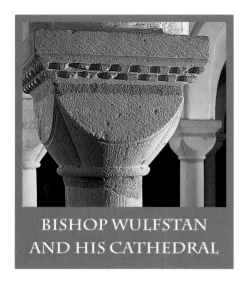

BISHOP WULFSTAN AND HIS CATHEDRAL

For many visitors this story begins in the Crypt, its vaulted roof and its slender, unadorned Norman pillars drawing the mind's eye back beyond the Crypt's thirteenth-century painting of an angel's face to the late eleventh century. Wulfstan (*c.*1009–1095) was educated at the monasteries of Evesham and Peterborough, became a monk at Worcester where he was elected Prior, and then, in 1062, became Bishop of Worcester. He was retained in this office by William I after the Norman Conquest four years later. An able and kind pastor, he was also an opponent of the slave trade in Bristol, built several new parish churches, and was the refounder of the monastery at Westbury-on-Trym. In 1084 he began the construction of a new cathedral at Worcester, replacing an earlier and simpler church which, like so many other monastic buildings in England, was partially destroyed when it fell victim to the Danish invaders of 1041. The height and length of Wulfstan's building were roughly those of the present building. Sadly not much of Wulfstan's cathedral now remains, a fact which makes the bases of the west door (visible outside the west door of the present cathedral) and the Crypt all the more special.

Below (and detail, above): The Crypt was begun by Wulfstan, re-using columns from an earlier building. Parts of the Crypt were filled in to support the new Quire and east end erected above it in the 13th century.

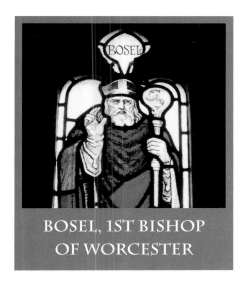

BOSEL, 1ST BISHOP OF WORCESTER

Wulfstan's cathedral was not the first cathedral in Worcester. Bosel, a Saxon, was consecrated as the first Bishop of Worcester in 680 by Theodore, Archbishop of Canterbury. With stone brought by river from local quarries such as those at Arley and Highley, Bosel began the building of the first cathedral in Worcester. Dedicated to the Apostle Peter, it stood for some three centuries. From the bishop's *cathedra*, the Latin term for 'seat', Bosel and his successors taught the Christian faith to the long-established and fortified town, situated on the high ground east of the river, and showed pastoral care to the people of the parishes of the diocese. Those teaching and pastoral responsibilities in all probability were both exciting and challenging, especially in Worcester itself. For Worcester, from earliest days, had been a centre of trade, travel and culture, the River Severn being a highway for trade and travel from both north and south. Commerce and passage from east and west were possible too, as the river was fordable at low tide and crossed by ferry at high tide. Of Bosel's cathedral church nothing remains, but his present successor still has his *cathedra* (the present one a nineteenth-century construction) in the Cathedral, and still exercises teaching and pastoral responsibilities towards all in the diocese.

Above: Detail of a depiction of Bishop Bosel from a 19th-century stained glass window in the east cloister.

Right: The Watergate dates from 1378 and held a defensive portcullis. Until the 19th century the River Severn flowed through this entrance at high tides.

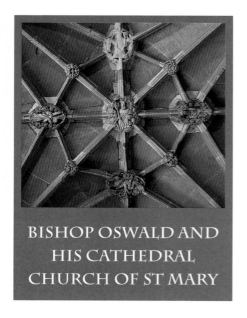

BISHOP OSWALD AND HIS CATHEDRAL CHURCH OF ST MARY

Between the cathedrals of Bosel and Wulfstan there was one other. Built alongside the old cathedral of Bosel and dedicated in 983 to the Blessed Virgin Mary, as noted in its Charter records, was the cathedral built by Oswald (c.925–992). Oswald came from a Danish family who had settled in England. At the direction of his uncle Odo, Archbishop of Canterbury, he had learned monastic discipline at the French abbey of Fleury. In 962 he was consecrated Bishop of Worcester, ten years before being made Archbishop of York – an office which he held whilst remaining Bishop of Worcester. In both dioceses he energetically sought to improve the standards of parochial clergy, fostering education and enforcing clerical celibacy – the latter a rather thankless task! Especially important was Oswald's role in the restoration of English monasticism. He founded the monastic community at Westbury-on-Trym, and established the community at Ramsey, from which were founded those at Pershore and Evesham. Two of these communities, those at Westbury-on-Trym and at Evesham, were, as we have noted, to be of importance for Wulfstan. Oswald also founded a monastic community in his new cathedral church of St Mary, to co-exist alongside the religious community in Bosel's cathedral church of St Peter next door.

The monastic community of St Mary's, like that based next door, followed the Rule of Benedict (c.480–c.547). The Rule combines insistence on good discipline with respect for human personality and individual capabilities, and is thoroughly practical. Benedict himself called his Rule one for beginners, a 'school of the Lord's service, in which we hope to order nothing harsh or rigorous'. The communities which followed the Rule were withdrawn from the world, but not isolated. The monks all slept in the Dormitory, sited beyond the west walk of the cloisters but now no longer standing. They washed communally in the same cloisters, where the *lavatorium*, to which fresh water from upstream of Worcester was piped, may still be seen. They ate in their Refectory, where the present College Hall, built over a Norman undercroft, now stands. They worked in the cloisters. Manuscripts such as Psalters and the Worcester Antiphoner (c.1230) – a unique record of the musical worship of a medieval monastery – were copied and illuminated in the clearer light of the east and south cloisters. Once completed, these were kept until the fourteenth century on wooden shelves in the 'cupboards' in the east cloister (where the late thirteenth- and fourteenth-century bells, one dedicated to Wulfstan, are now on display). The Cathedral's literary treasures now are held in the Cathedral Library where they are conserved for use by people from across the world.

The monks met in the Chapter House to discuss and decide matters relating to their common life – the present early twelfth-century one, a prototype of those at Wells and Lincoln, has seating 'in the round' as an aid to conversation and a statement to the value of all opinions. They prayed in the Quire of the Cathedral. Their sense of mercy for all, and of God's mercy for them, is epitomised in the *misericords*, the seats for the monks. These seats could be upturned to reveal underneath a support insufficient in itself to bear the weight of a monk, but

Above: 14th-century stone bosses sculpted in the ceiling ribs of the south cloister vault. The figures and foliage represent the Tree of Jesse and were originally painted.

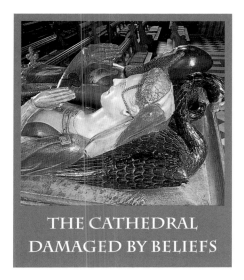

THE CATHEDRAL
DAMAGED BY BELIEFS

With the death of Prince Arthur came change. Arthur's younger brother became King Henry VIII, and the English Reformation duly followed. The Cathedral itself endured, but all else seems to have altered. In 1540 the Benedictine monastery was dissolved, the shrines of Saints Oswald and Wulfstan having previously been destroyed and their bodies reburied in unknown places. Under Dean Barlow (a successor according to the new Cathedral constitution to Henry Holbeche, who was both the last Prior of the monastery and first Dean of the Cathedral), the screens across the Nave were destroyed, the monks' stalls were removed, and stained glass windows were either taken away or defaced. A large number of statues were damaged too – the damage done to the sculptured east wall of Prince Arthur's chantry is still visible. Wall paintings were scraped off, or covered with whitewash, as is still clear in the north Quire aisle, Chapter House, Lady's Chapel and Dean's Chapel.

Above (detail): The tomb of Sir John and Lady Joan Beauchamp of Powick in the north aisle. Their heads rest on black swans, which appear on their coat of arms.

Below: On the flat wall between the carved spandrels in the Dean's Chapel, painted halos and faces of saints, destroyed in the 16th century, are just visible.

Left: The painted effigies of Robert and Margaret Wylde lie in prayer on their tomb. Robert, a merchant, died in 1607.

Below: Detail of a 19th-century window from the north cloister walk, depicting scenes from the time of Chaucer (author of *The Canterbury Tales*) and Wycliffe, who translated the Bible into English.

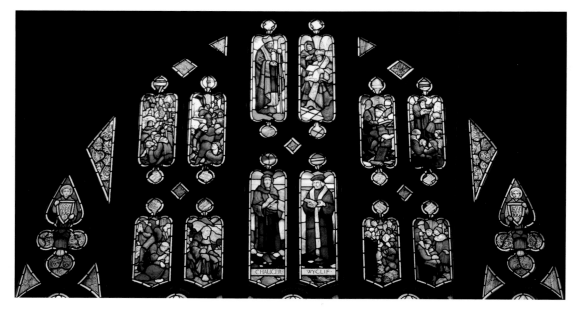

Right: The 13th-century St George Chapel now houses many military memorials.

Below: The Cathedral Choir, scholars of the King's School, sing services daily in term time, and also perform, tour and make recordings of their music.

No wonder that the people of the present-day Cathedral community also celebrate the architects and archaeologist, the carpenters and caterers, and cleaners and electricians, the gardeners and glaziers, the masons and librarians, the plumbers and roofers, those who welcome the visitors, and those who lock up in the evening. For as Oswald and Wulfstan and the many Benedictines of the past believed, so those of today still believe that to work is to pray and to pray is to work.

Right: A member of the Cathedral's Flower Guild.

Below: The stonemasons use the same techniques as their Medieval and Victorian forebears to repair and restore the Cathedral. The stone boss (left) is a 'practice piece' on which they would learn their craft.

The 19th-century font, a
reminder of our own baptism.

The ceiling above the high altar shows Christ in Glory surrounded by the Heavenly Host. It was designed by George Gilbert Scott and painted by Hardman's.

The Quire ceiling was designed by George Gilbert Scott and painted by Hardman's. It is covered with medallions of saints and angels.

ACKNOWLEDGEMENTS

The Chapter of Worcester Cathedral acknowledges the special help given by Barbara Dollery, Alvyn Pettersen and Janet Sinclair in the preparation of this guide.